RAF Burtonwood
50 Years of

1. A Republic F-84F Thunders... aircraft was truly supersonic wi... underwing ordnance load of 6,0... to Burtonwood for major servic...

...F-86 Sabre this ...t could carry an ...nan bases came

...oto: Roger Bate

Aldon P Ferguson

First published 1989 by
Airfield Publications
18 Ridge Way
Wargrave
Berkshire RG10 8AS

Reprinted 1998

ISBN 0 951111 31 0

Printed in Great Britain by
J.W. Arrowsmith Ltd., Bristol

2. June 1944. Police vehicles escort a convoy of Burtonwood bound aircraft as they are towed out of Liverpool Docks. The building and bridges in the background belong to the now long defunct Liverpool Overhead Railway.

Photo: Flight

Foreword

The compilation of this book is a direct result of the feedback from my first book on Burtonwood *Eighth Air Force Base Air Depot – RAF Burtonwood* which was published in 1986. I was overwhelmed by the response and feedback from men and women who were based there and who showed such a loving affection for Burtonwood and the Warrington area. The original book opened up a wealth of additional material and I amassed hundreds of new photographs. The wholesale demolition of the base since 1986 has changed the landscape beyond recognition and therefore it is timely to remember what was there before the entire airfield site is redeveloped by the Warrington and Runcorn Development Corporation.

Burtonwood was probably the largest military base in Europe during World War Two, processing over 11,500 aircraft between 1943 and 1945 alone, but beyond that it was responsible for the support of initially the 8th Air Force, then additionally the 9th and ultimately the 12th and 15th Air Forces as well. Over 35,000 men were under the direct control of Burtonwood with 18,500 on the base itself. Nothing was too big or small, from rebuilding battle damaged bombers to manufacturing valve springs for aero engines, manufacturing timber packing cases or converting gliders into powered aircraft.

After World War Two Burtonwood returned to the RAF for two years as a maintenance unit and then reverted to the USAF in 1948 to support the US bases here, and it undertook all the major servicing for the C-54 Skymaster aircraft involved in the Berlin Airlift. Major redevelopment took place with the construction of the Header House on Site 8, the extension of the runway to 9,000ft to be one of the longest in the UK and the construction of the new control tower and passenger terminal. After eleven years of maximum use the mission reduced and by 1965 the base passed back to RAF control. Two years later, however, the US Army took command and remain there to this day, albeit occupying only a fraction of the original site.

Much has been demolished and the main runway now forms the base of the M62 motorway but I hope that this book will graphically illustrate what a huge and important base RAF Burtonwood was, and will serve as a memory to all those who have had the privilege to be stationed there, those who had their part to play in the Burtonwood Story.

RAF Burtonwood celebrates its Fiftieth Anniversary on 1st April 1990.

Aldon P Ferguson
November 1989

Acknowledgements

The compilation of this book of photographs would not have been possible without the support, encouragement, knowledge and collection of Colonel Walter W "Dewey" Ott USAF (Retired) who has the superb collection of photographs given to his cousin General Ike W Ott, who was commanding officer of Base Air Depot Area, Burtonwood, from 1943 to 1945. This magnificent set of photographs is spread throughout the book.

Chris Stride has taken my rough negatives and turned them into superb prints of all sizes and many, many of his prints are reproduced herein. For his hours of patient work I am indebted .

I must also thank Roger Bate and Phil Butler who had the foresight in the 1950s to take as many photographs as they could, with security still tight; Ron Oldacre who was a base photographer in the mid-1950s and who sensibly kept copies of the more interesting photographs he took; and to the many members of the Burtonwood Association who have so freely opened up their private photograph collections to me allowing me to copy whatever I wanted.

I have tried to give due credit to the originator of every photograph but inevitably some slip through the net. To everyone who has helped and encouraged me I owe you a great deal of thanks and my apologies to anyone I have mistakenly omitted.

Finally, nothing would have been possible if it was not for my wife, Sue, who has accompanied me on numerous trips to Burtonwood and the United States and allowed me time to compile this book and supported me throughout.

To you all — my sincere thanks.

3. An early aerial photograph of Burtonwood taken from a height of about 5,000 ft on 7 September 1942 just as the first US troops arrived. Looking south west towards Tech Site the newly built main runway can be clearly seen, not yet camouflaged, running top right to lower centre. The other two runways were built in 1940 and have been painted in an attempt to disguise them from the air. The new loop taxiway to the west end of the runway looks new and the extension to the north end of Runway 33 has not been completed. Note the only living site is Site 6 behind Tech Site with no evidence of Site 1 or 2. The hangars of Mary Ann Site *centre left* are camouflaged but there is no hardstanding in front of this site or Tech Site. Aircraft can be seen on the original photograph around the hangars of A Site in the bottom right corner. Tracks to dispersals can just be discerned running under the cloud bottom centre and also into a field just below Mary Ann Site. Note how rural the area appears with nothing but farms surrounding the base. BRD Site is off the picture to the left.

Photo: RAF Museum

4. Another view from the same series as the one above taken looking south with BRD Site in the centre background. The new main runway is running bottom right to centre left. In the right foreground are the three "L" type hangars of E Site. The River Mersey can be seen top right and the track linking BRD Site with Mary Ann Site can also be seen running along the route of what was later named "The Burma Road".

Photo: RAF Museum

5. The churned-up mud in the foreground shows the intense use of the entire base for operations. A B-17 lands in front of the mobile controller's "caravan" at the upwind end of the runway. This brightly painted vehicle was positioned to allow a controller to visually inspect every landing and taking-off aircraft to ensure that the undercarriage was down and there were no abnormalities.

Photo: Col Walter W Ott

6. An oblique view from the north west corner of the airfield looking across the main runway towards Tech Site with Lithgoe Site behind. B-24 Liberators are parked on the taxiway in the foreground with a mixture of B-17s, C-47s and P-47s spread across the main ramp and on the inactive runway (09-27). The wartime control tower can be seen in front of the J type hangars of Tech Site.

Photo: Col Walter W Ott

7. Dispersals full of B-24s in this view looking across from Mary Ann Site towards the north and A Site. The B-24s occupy "spectacle" type hardstandings; note some are in bare metal and others painted. Lined up on the grass are 20 P-47 Thunderbolts whilst more Liberators can be seen waiting outside the hangars of A Site. The canvas awning to break up the line of the hangars can be clearly seen.

Photo: Col Walter W Ott

8. Tinker Hall Site from the air in 1944. This shot is taken from the south west of the airfield looking north east. In the immediate foreground are the black nissen huts of Site 6 with the storage shed and three Bellman hangars bottom right and the end of the Lamella hangar on E Site bottom left. In the centre are hangars J and K on Tech Site with the original RAF camp immediately in front of it. To the right can be seen one of the aircraft hardstandings with a mixture of B-17s, B-24s, C-47s and others. Top centre are the two J type hangars of A Site used initially by Rootes Securities, then the RAF, then Flight Test and finally as production hangars. After the war they acted as the trans-Atlantic terminal and housed C-54 Skymasters undergoing 200 hour overhauls for the Berlin Airlift (Operation Vittles). In 1989 they still remain more or less intact and are utilised for grain and container storage.

Photo: Bill Thomas

9. The Mary Ann Site ramp on 18 May 1957 with a Fairchild C-119 Packet. The C-119 had two Wright R-3350-32W engines giving it a top speed of 296 mph and a range of 3,480 miles—enough to reach the UK from the States. With 59th Air Depot Group supporting the whole USAF in Britain it was inevitable that transport aircraft were constantly on the move in and out of Burtonwood to and from the States and other bases in Britain and the continent.

Photo: Roger Bate

10. Taken from the top of the "new" tower across the ramp of Tech Site looking east towards Mary Ann Site in the distance, this view shows a Fairchild C-123B Provider in the foreground, a Douglas C-124 Globemaster in the centre and a Douglas C-118 in the background used for short range cargo, long range cargo and long range passengers respectively. The hangar in the foreground is hangar "J".

Photo: Ron Oldacre

11. Another view from the same position in 1956 with two C-119s in the foreground serialled 12639 and 25923 respectively. Beyond left are two C-124 Globemaster transport aircraft and the ramp shows a mixture of C-118s and C-47s. A total of fifteen transport aircraft can be seen which is normal for any day in the 1950s.

Photo: Dr A A Duncan

12. The same view taken in 1976 with the ramps deserted, Burtonwood totally unused except for gliders and the coal mining beginning to make itself felt under Mary Ann Site. The C type hangars of Mary Ann Site can be seen in the distance.

Photo: Aldon P Ferguson

13. Possibly the crew of the last MATS flight out of Burtonwood carrying passengers which took place in 1959. Colonel W W Ott, captain, is on the left with the rest of the crew of eight. The aircraft is a Douglas C-188.

Photo: Col Walter W Ott

14. The second control tower to be constructed at Burtonwood. This standard RAF tower was positioned in front of Tech Site in 1942 as the original Fort type was badly positioned after the construction of runway 09-27, as the approach to 27 was obscured by Tech Site hangars. The site of the first tower was required as aircraft hardstanding and it was demolished. This tower remained the major tower for aircraft control from 1942 to 1953 when it was replaced by the new, much taller, tower immediately behind. It was still used as the communications HQ and standby tower and was only demolished in 1987. This picture was taken in the early 1950s.

Photo: Andy Skiba

15. The wartime tower was a standard RAF 12775/41 type, built of brick with two storeys and a control room on top. The building to the right has a sign over the door unfortunately just indiscernible on the original—but there is a seat outside with four men sitting on it waiting for something to happen! This tower remained in use until 1953 when it was superceded by the new tall tower.

Photo: Carl J Winkleman

16. Airman Burkhalter using the fixed Aldis lamp in the local control at the top of the 1953 control tower on Tech Site. Burtonwood was, and still is, in the Manchester Control Zone and all movements of aircraft were co-ordinated with Speke, Ringway and Stretton Royal Navy airbase.

Photo: Burtonwood Beacon

17. A view inside the wartime control tower on Tech Site showing the cramped conditions in which the controllers had to work. This was the "cabin" housed on the roof containing local control which controlled aircraft on the ground, taxiing and on final approach or taking off. Approach control, in the more spacious room immediately below, looked after aircraft approaching and leaving the airfield. This tower was superceded in 1953 by the newer one

Photo: Burtonwood Beacon

18. The standard RAF wartime tower constructed in 1942 opposite to Tech Site and used throughout the war up to 1953 when it was superceded by the new tower seen behind. This house-like structure constructed to Air Ministry drawing No 12779/41 contained the Watch Office, Met Office and rest room on the ground floor with the Control Room, Signals Office and Controllers Rest Room on the first floor. The control room on the roof varied from station to station and was usually constructed to local requirements. At Burtonwood the control room became the approach room and local control of aircraft and vehicles on the ground was monitored from the roof-top room. This building became the radio centre once the new tower was built and was kept in good order until the mid-1960s when it was left to decay.

Photo: Aldon P Ferguson

19. A poor quality photograph taken from a contemporary copy of the Burtonwood Beacon in 1953 showing the 1953 control under construction. Over 80 ft high this tower gave a commanding view across the sprawling base and allowed the controllers to clearly see the ends of the main runway and aircraft taxiing anywhere on the airfield together with vehicles on the airfield. The new terminal building was constructed simultaneously housing everything a small airport should contain. Access to the top of the tower was by means of a series of vertical ladders and the intermediate landings housed batteries for emergency use in the event of power failure.

20. Desolate hardstandings taken in the 1970s showing hangar J on Tech Site with the newer control tower and terminal building underneath. The terminal contained customs, American Express, news stand, lounge, immigration and emigration, and had everything a small airport should have. The last passenger flight departed in 1959 and the tower was eventually demolished on 17 April 1988.

Photo: Aldon P Ferguson

21. The first Ground Controlled Approach (GCA) truck at Burtonwood in the late 40s. Using primitive wartime radar this unit could guide aircraft down to the runway in very poor visibility. It was replaced by the more modern unit below.

22. The later GCA trailer positioned near the end of the runway in use in the 1950s. Only one set was available and it was moved to the upwind end of the runway in use as necessary. The trailer was in direct control with the landing aircraft and the control tower.

23. Evocative view of the wet ramp at Burtonwood epitomising the view so many newly arrived servicemen and their families enjoyed then they first landed on British soil. The photo was taken adjacent to the "Local" control room on the RAF 12779/41 tower looking across the roof to the 1953 tower and terminal – once "The Gateway to Europe" – which is alas no more. February 1982.

Photo: Aldon P Ferguson

24. Site 1 (Colin Kelly Hall) from the air in 1944. Burtonwood Road runs across the bottom of the photograph from right to left and the orientation is looking east. The original farm can be seen to the lower left of the site and the usual nissen and temporary timber hutting can be seen. In the centre are the Mess Hall and the Aero Club (Seco-hutting) later to become the Elementary and High Schools for dependants. The site was demolished in the 1960s. In the background are B-17 Fortress bombers awaiting attention lying in one of the many dispersals. Once the main runway was enlarged in 1953 this site was located in the middle of the airfield.

Photo: Bill Thomas

25. B-24 Liberators lined up on the dispersal near No 1 Site awaiting attention. Note the Robin hangar in the left foreground. Built by the RAF for fighter aircraft this building has three false chimneys on its roof in a vain attempt to disguise it from German reconnaissance aircraft.

Photo: Col Walter W Ott

26. An aerial view of the dispersal near No 1 Site showing gleaming new B-17s fresh from their trans-Atlantic flight into Burtonwood. Nearly thirty can be seen here none yet with squadron codes or markings. In winter these dispersals turned to mud and hard-core tracks had to be provided to prevent these heavy bombers from sinking into the ground.

Photo: Col Walter W Ott

27. The derelict entrance to Site 1 taken in about 1960 showing a sign advising "Private – Keep Out". Still intact at this time it was becoming vandalised and was home to a few squatters. Too far gone for refurbishment these wartime "Temporary" buildings enjoyed a 20 year life prior to demolition.

28. Neat lines of nissen huts on Site 2 in June 1957. Well appointed with paved footpaths, fences and landscaped areas this is a far cry from the areas of mud endured in wartime days.

Photo: Donald Squibb

29. *Below:* Going for chow at the Site 2 (Wagner Hall) Mess Hall in May 1945.

Photo: Carl E Hewgley

33. *Opposite page:* The Site 5 (Billy Mitchell Hall) Mess Hall was customized for the GIs and had bulletin boards displayed outside to show how the war was going and the activities on the site that day. This picture shows the main entrance with the prop and board to the left with the headline "600 Super Forts hit Japan" under the heading "Special Victory Drive Flashes" and there is a map of the far east to the right. Note the bombs and fins painted white to mark the path in the dark. The board to the right gives details of movies, theatre, sports, dances and religion with the latest athletics information displayed below.

Photo: Carl J Winkleman

30. The main Base Exchange or PX on Site 4 selling US goods and including a snack bar. The cars identify the date as May 1957.

Photo: Donald Squibb

31. *Below:* Reflecting the most common item on the wartime menu The Spamteria was the Mess Hall on Site 5. The English girls were no doubt the cooks and kitchen staff. Todays menu reads:— Meat Loaf and Gravy, boiled potatoes, buttered beets, onions, spice, bread and butter, jam and coffee.

Photo: Carl J Winkleman

32. *Below right:* Ed Swinney drew this cartoon depicting the GIs' view of Burtonwood weather! Ed was editor of the *Burtonwood Beacon* for several years.

34. A close-up of the board featured on previous page.

Photo: Carl J Winkleman

35. Another shot of the news board outside the Mess Hall reading that peace is almost agreed in the far east and that there are no US Air Force operations today. It also states that the War Dept has restricted the flying of the P-80 Shooting Star, one of which had recently exploded in the air over Burtonwood, killing the pilot.

Photo: Carl J Winkleman

Another close-up at the Mess Hall showing the prop with "Bill Mit-Chell ll" written thereon together with a badge on the boss which is the 8th Air rce badge doctored with a "BM" in the middle for Billy Mitchell. Note the ntemporary bicycle.

Photo: Carl J Winkleman

37. The Site 5 Library operated by Special Services. This has been converted from a standard nissen hut. The tin outside is for cigarette butts.

Photo: Carl J Winkleman

38. Another view of the Site 5 Library and Chapel in adjacent huts.

Photo: Carl J Winkleman

39. The main entrance to Site 5 in July 1957 showing men just leaving the bus stop and the covered curved shelter at the bus stop just to the left of the sign board. Each site was self contained with mess hall and most had their own cinema.

Photo: Donald Squibb

40. The original RAF huts comprised the first living site to be known as Site 6. Initially only having earth tracks linking them the resultant mud made a hard surface essential. Site 6 was enlarged by the USAAF immediately after arrival by the construction of approximately sixty nissen huts. Due to the location close to Tech Site and the superior nature of construction they were used throughout the life of the base by officers and after the war by officers and their families.

Photo: Arthur L Smith

41. A view of Site 6 on Tinker Hall in 1945 showing the typical nissen huts used for accommodation on all sites. Looking north east the original farm house can be seen in the distance that was requisitioned and used as the home of Brig General Ike Ott. Due to intense use and frequent rain, concrete pathways had to be laid to get rid of the constant mud.

Photo: Maurice E Hale Jr

42. The rear of the Officers' Club on Site 6 showing the post-war extension to give more room for functions which were on every night of the week, seven days a week. 28 April 1957.

Photo: Donald Squibb

43. One of the early RAF buildings on Site 6 converted into senior officers' living accommodation in the 1950s. This was one of the few brick constructed buildings not on Tech or BRD Sites. October 1957.

Photo: Donald Squibb

44. Another view inside hangar AD4, 5 or 6 on Mary Ann Site. AD stands for "Aircraft Dock" and each hangar had two crews for the two shifts. Jealous but friendly rivalry prevailed between the ADs or hangars as each strove to produce more aircraft than its neighbour in a given time period. Here B-24 Liberators are being stripped of their armament and weight and painted black for the "Carpetbagger" programme for clandestine operations over occupied Europe.

45. An aerial view of Tech Site as existing in 1976. The writing on the roof of hangar "J" is clearly visible and reads: "Burtonwood Army Airfield – Elev 70". The new tower and terminal can be seen in front of the hangar together with the twin hangar "K". The main brick buildings are still standing but the buildings of No 6 Site behind are now demolished with only the roads still remaining.

Photo: Aldon P Ferguson

46. Another photo taken at the same time as the one above showing the alignment of the M62 motorway which links Manchester and Liverpool and crosses the Pennines to Leeds and Hull. The motorway is aligned on the main runway (09-27) and the perimeter track can be seen top right. The bases of Tinker Hall Site incorporating Sites 6 and G and Lythgoe can be clearly seen top left. The wartime tower is positioned bottom centre and the extended hardstanding forming the ramp outside the terminal is still in good condition in 1976.

Photo: Aldon P Ferguson

47. The passenger and crew entrance to the Tech Site passenger terminal on 29 September 1957 with the contemporary sign above. The reflection of a C-47 can be seen in the glass window.

Photo: Donald Squibb

48. Another sign in almost the same location but taken in 1976 shows that the base is now firmly under US Army control.

Photo: Aldon P Ferguson

49. The interior of a standard nissen hut of which 1,054 existed in the 1950s—it is estimated that there were originally over 2,000 on the base. Here the men of Maintenance Division made special fitted cupboards for their personal belongings. Clearly cleaned up for inspection this picture shows how fourteen beds could be arranged with the two central ones parallel to the walls to keep away from the single stove placed in the centre. With virtually no insulation these buildings were freezing in winter.

Photo: John R Diehr

50. A magnificent vertical photograph taken on 10 August 1945, five days before VE-Day. The photograph graphically illustrates the hard use of the base with the ground churned up everywhere. The hardstandings can be seen outside Tech and Mary Ann Sites and aircraft can be seen all the way around the perimeter track, mostly awaiting scrapping. External storage can be seen all around the hangars of G Site and the warehouses on Mary Ann and No 6 Sites. The twin tails of surplus P-38 Lightnings can be spotted on the dispersal immediately above Mary Ann Site.

Photo: Crown Copyright

51. Aerial view of the centre of the airfield taken on 20 August 1959 by the RAF. The newer areas of concrete between Tech and Mary Ann Sites are very obvious but the total lack of aircraft or vehicles show that the USAF have all but pulled out and the airfield is left to graze with very few aircraft movements. Bottom centre is No 2 Site with the baseball pitches immediately above. No 7 Site (in ruins) is on bottom right and No 1 Site centre right. The storage warehouses at Mary Ann Site can be clearly seen as can those on G Site. The crosses on the two cross runways indicate that they are now disused. Unfortunately the end of the main runway (09-27) cannot be seen.

Photo: Crown Copyright

52. The airfield on 16 May 1973 with the construction of the M62 motorway along the main runway taking place. By now the warehouses on Mary Ann and No 6 Sites have been demolished with only their concrete bases visible. On most sites only bases of huts remain and wholesale demolition has got well under way. The double "H" shape at the bottom of No 2 Site is the floor of the base hospital (200 beds) and the bridge over the motorway can be seen with the beginning of the service area to its right.

Photo: Aerofilms Ltd

53. Headquarters Northern Air Materiel Area on Tech Site in May 1957. Used as the HQ building also during WWII this building remained until 1987 when it was demolished.

Photo: Donald Squibb

54. Gunnery trainer as seen in March 1980 located on the west side of Tech Site. Designed to train RAF aerial gunners it is a strange building to have on this base as it usually was only seen on gunnery training stations.

Photo: Aldon P Ferguson

55. Building No 35 on Tech Site, a standard RAF type HQ building used in the 1950s as the Wing HQ.

Photo: Aldon P Ferguson

56. Similar in design to Building No 35, building No 36 was a Group HQ building.

Photo: Aldon P Ferguson

57. Photographed just prior to demolition in October 1986 this Seco type building was a late addition to building No 35.

Photo: Aldon P Ferguson

58. Another photo of the rear of the Wing HQ taken in March 1980.

Photo: Aldon P Ferguson

59. Originally the RAF Stores, building No 32 was later used as Base Post Office, Base Finance and Bank.

Photo: Aldon P Ferguson

60. The MT Section on Tech Site photographed in March 1980. Woefully small for future use it was the standard RAF design for Maintenance Units and survived until the end in 1986.

Photo: Aldon P Ferguson

61. The Transient Hotel was a Seco type building located on Lythgoe Site for overnight accommodation for visiting flight crews. July 1957.

Photo: Donald Squibb

62. Often the first building entered by new personnel this building was the processing station for personnel entering or leaving Europe. Photographed on Lythgoe Site in July 1957.

Phot: Donald Squibb

63. Burtonwood Repair Depot (BRD) from the air in 1944. Note the camouflage on the buildings, the engine test houses top left, the railway lines running down the entire rear of the site and the marshalling yards to the top. BRD Site was a factory capable of making anything from propellers, plexi-glass canopies, bomb slings, etc. This site was responsible for overhauling 30,386 aero engines in WWII, servicing items like 2,476,462 spark plugs and checking and packing 71,442 parachutes.

Photo: Bill Thomas

64. An excellent wartime aerial view of BRD Site looking east towards Warrington. The two rows of workshops were camouflaged and some of the aircraft can be seen in the bottom left hand corner. The engine test houses are top left and the goods yard running directly off British Railways can be seen top right. The road in the bottom foreground is Burtonwood Road running to the airfield off to the left.

Photo: Bill Thomas

N

65. **BRD** Site from the south in 1960 with the extensive railway marshalling yard in the foreground together with the spur running across Burtonwood Road to the Header House. The engine test houses are still standing but the open ones beyond have now been demolished. The "H" shaped building at the entrance to BRD Site is the HQ and the "A" type hangar on this site can be seen in the top left corner. Out on the airfield the hardstanding outside Mary Ann Site can be seen utilised for storage.

Photo: US Army

66-67. Two shots of BRD Site as seen in March 1983 showing the main production buildings still in good condition maintained by the Department of the Environment as a Government Store. The smaller workshops and living and mess building have been mostly removed but, with the exception of a fire in 1965 which destroyed the south end of the building, the site remains essentially the same as it was in 1943.

Photo: Aldon P Ferguson

68. The A type hangar on BRD Site stands still opposite the main gate to the US Army base. This hangar was once known as Site 10 when there was chronic shortage of accommodation and 1,000 men lived in here for three months whilst their huts were being built – very convenient for work! This hangar also housed aircraft and training aids for No 21 School of Technical Training, RAF, and many training airframes were parked around the area. Photographed in March 1983 this building remains in good order and would have been taken back by the US Army for additional storage but for US defence budget cuts.

Photo: Aldon P Ferguson

69. Not only were the aircraft named but many of the "Homes" were also christened by their inmates. Idiot's Retreat was home to Herschel Grey and nine others in 1944-45.

Photo: Herschel Grey

70. A Standard 16ft span nissen hut sporting four swastikas on the door. It may be the living accommodation of PFC Arthur Seher of the 890th Military Police Company (Aviation), who apprehended four German prisoners of war who had escaped from a camp in Northwich and were hiding in a B-26 Marauder in a dispersal, on Saturday 9th December 1944. The Germans were hoping to get the aircraft started and to fly home for Christmas. The flicker of a match betrayed their presence and they were arrested and returned to their camp.

Photo: Carl J Winkleman

71. A winter scene from the top of the new tow[er] looking out across the snow to the wartime tow[er] now, in 1958, used as the radio room and shop.
Photo: Donald Squib[b]

72. The main entrance to Bruche Hall living site located on the east of Warrington. This self contained site had accommodation for about 2,000 personnel and a regular bus and truck run connected the site with Burtonwood. With so many personnel on the base it was impossible to accommodate them all so this old British Army base was taken over, together with Canada Hall at Padgate.

Photo: Ted Wurm

73. The central activity hall on Bruche Hall Sit[e] used as a dance hall, assembly hall, theatr[e] cinema or social centre. Photo taken from th[e] officers quarters area in July 1942.
Photo: Ted Wur[m]

74. The Sunnyside Hotel in Southport, Lancashire. Requisitioned by the US forces who also requisitioned other hotels, such as the Imperial, for office use. This hotel was the centre of operations for Base Air Depot Area which controlled BAD's 1, 2 and 3 at Burtonwood, Warton and Langford Lodge, Northern Ireland, respectively. HQ BADA moved with its commander General Ike Ott to Burtonwood in March 1944. The hotel continued as offices for the US Army and ultimately became the Southport American Red Cross Club after the closure of the Palace Hotel at Birkdale which had been the main centre.
The hotel reverted to British use shortly after the end of hostilities and is now a convalescent home.

Photo: Col Walter W Ott

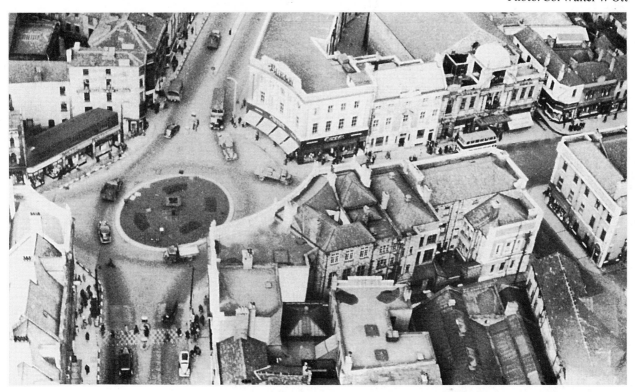

75. An aerial view taken in 1945 from a very low flying US aircraft over the centre of Warrington. The Empire theatre can be seen top right and Burtons tailors on the corner. The early type of zebra crossing can be seen bottom left.

Photo: Col William Clement

76. A wintry scene at Bewsey Bridge over the St Helens canal. This small bridge linked Sites 4 and 5 with Warrington and was used every day both during and after the war as a short cut to the pubs and girls of Warrington. In 1989 it is still there although in a more permanently fixed state.

78. The centre of Warrington as seen through the camera of Bill Shahan in 1945.
Photo: Bill Shahan

77. Looking from the Sankey Street American Red Cross Club towards the central roundabout in the heart of Warrington, 1944. Note the total lack of traffic due to wartime fuel restrictions.

Photo: J R Zeller

The Men

79. 2nd Air Depot Group arrived at Burtonwood from Molesworth in June 1942 having recently arrived in the UK. In September it was disbanded as a separate unit and was amalgamated with 5th Air Depot Group and other units to form Base Air Depot No 1.

Photo: Ernest J Smith

80. *Below:* Men of Flight Test on a wet cold day at Burtonwood in 1945. They are sitting on a B-17, one of the 4,243 to pass through the base in just under two years. Flight Test received the aircraft from Maintenance Division and after careful pre-flight checks and engine runs they took each aircraft up for a test flight before signing that it was ready for delivery. Delivery flights were undertaken by one of the ferry squadrons or sometimes by Flight Test or pilots of the recipient unit. With bad weather prevalent many aircraft would back up for flights and it was important to get them delivered as quickly as possible. A full list of names of the men is available but is too big to reproduce here.

Photo: George Finlay

82. PFC's Osborne, Joe Mobile and George Lintz on Site 2 in 1944.
Photo: Foster F Ma

81. *Left:* A group of men outside a standard nissen hut somewhere on Burtonwo
Left to right: Hearn, T X; Lindenberger, N J; Lloyd Steele, C A; Deluca, N J; Tol
T X; Warner, W I; Chamberlain, N J and Moyes, P A.
Photo: Lloyd St

83. The Signals section of BAD1 photographed on a B-17 on 27 October 1944.
Photo: Bill Tho

4. A "Supply Expediter" motor scooter essential for getting around the vast base waiting to speed off for spares outside a J Type hangar on A Site in 1944.

Photo: John R Diehr

5. *Right:* This picture tells all on VE-Day. Suddenly the role of Burtonwood had been successfully filled and time was spent celebrating prior to returning to work for the defeat of Japan.

Photo: Carl E Hewgley

6. The 1,000th 'bird' to pass through BAD1. The tail of this B-17 is covered with the men from hangar AD-6 on Mary Ann Site who worked on her in 1944. Note one finger raised to illustrate 1,000

Photo: James M Albers Jr

87. Line up of men from Tiffin AFB in the States serving at Burtonwood in 1944.

Photo: Frank Zeller

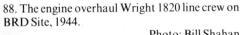

88. The engine overhaul Wright 1820 line crew on BRD Site, 1944.

Photo: Bill Shahan

89. A tribute to all the photographers who have contributed to this book. This shows Ron Oldacre (*right*) about to climb into a Standard Vanguard shooting brake provided by the British to go to a photograph engagement. The Base Photo Lab on Tech Site, once the Decontamination centre, was home to up to 32 personnel dealing with the photographic needs of Burtonwood. In the late 1940s and 1950s the lab processed over 50,000 photographs a year depicting all aspects of life from road accidents to carnival queens, from fires to Father Christmas entertaining the local children in the base clubs at Christmas. Unfortunately the negatives were sorted out annually and those not required (the majority) were burned! The Lab was manned 24 hours a day 365 days a year ready to record any event and employed both service and civilian personnel.

Photo: Ron Oldacre

90. A posed shot for *Pathe News* taken just prior to D-Day (6th June 1944) showing a line up of Burtonwood prepared P-47 Thunderbolts ready for delivery already with invasion stripes painted under their wings and fuselages. *Left to right:* General I W Ott, Commander BADA; General William H "Billy" Arnold, Chief of Maintenance; Major W W "Dewey" Ott, Chief Flight Test; and behind is Sgt Albers, General Ott's chauffeur.

Photo: Colonel Walter W Ott

91. General I W "Ike" Ott, Commander Base Air Depot Area (BADA) initially at Kelly Field, TX, then at Southport, Lancashire and moved across to Burtonwood on 6 March 1944.
Photo: Colonel Walter W Ott

92. In June 1953 Brigadier General Troup Miller Jr arrived from the USA via Bremerhaven and air to Burtonwood to take command of the then 59th Air Depot Wing. Colonel Dan H Yeilding (*right*) Chief of Staff greeted the new commander. Arriving with the General were his wife and three daughters, Judy, Marilyn and Latherine. A native of Atlanta, GA, Brig Gen Miller was named executive officer in the Office of Deputy Chief of Staff for Materiel, HQ USAF in February 1951.   Photo: Colonel Walter W Ott

93. In January 1950, the two immediate commanders to precede Brig General Troup Miller, NAMA Commander, met as they transferred command. Brig General and Mrs Robert C Oliver and son, Bob, (*left*) newly arrived, were greeted by Major General and Mrs Samuel A Anderson, departing for the US.

Photo: Burtonwood Beacon

94. Colonel Alton A Denton became Chief of Staff, NAMA, Burtonwood in August 1953, replacing Colonel Dan H Yeilding.

Photo: Burtonwood Beacon

95. Brig General Troup Miller Jr, commander of NAMA and NAMAE from June 1953 to June 1956.

Photo: Burtonwood Beacon

96. Colonel Graves H Snyder was Burtonwood's Base Commander for two years from June 1956 to June 1958. He was replaced by Lt Col L R Kittel.

Photo: Burtonwood Beacon

Colonel Edwin J Hamilton, Base Commander
1958 to May 1959.

Photo: Burtonwood Beacon

98. Always a Royal Air Force base, Burtonwood
has an RAF commander. In August 1950 Wing
Commander A E Harbot, MBE, assumed
command.

99. Colonel John R Moran, US Army, assumed
command on 24 August 1987 and left for
Germany in August 1989.

100. Brig General James G Bickford *(right)* officially handing over command to Colonel James G Kalanges *(left)* on 29 May 1986. In the centre is
Lt General John D Bruen, Commander 21st Support Command in Germany.

101. General Jacob L Devers (*right*) Commander US Forces Europe until succeeded by General Eisenhower in December 1943. Major General Hugh Miller (*centre*) seen with a British civilian on Mary Ann Site 1943.

Photo: Col Walter W Ott

102. General Dwight David "Ike" Eisenhower (1890-1969) on an official vi just prior to D-Day (6th June 1944). On Ike's left is General Ike O Commander BADA and on his left, face only of General Hugh Mill General "Tooey" Spaatz (with glasses) and Colonel William H "Bil Arnold looking away (Chief of Maintenance). Gen Spaatz was command in-chief of the US strategic air force in the UK.   Photo: Col Walter W O

103. General George Patton (*right*) arriving at HQ on BRD Site in April 1944. The saluting civilian is Donald Nelson, US Chief of War Production with Major General Hugh Knerr behind and Brig General I W Ott immediately in front of the MP. Note the hooded headlights on the staff car.

Photo: Col Walter W Ott

4. General Henry Harley "Hep" Arnold (1886-1950) arriving at urtonwood in 1943 shaking hands with Colonel Billy Arnold. *Left to right:* nknown, Colonel Jim Lancing, Major General Hugh Miller, General Ike t, Unknown (almost concealed), Colonel Bill Brittan, Colonel Wilson, ad of Administration and Colonel William H "Billy" Arnold.

Photo: Col Walter W Ott

105. General George Smith Patton (1885-1945) seen alighting from his personal C-47 at Burtonwood in 1944 on an inspection and consultation just prior to D-Day. General Patton had his Third Army HQ at Knutsford for some time prior to D-Day not actually landing in France until 6 July 1944 and then having to wait for his newly activated Army to catch up with him. Patton did not enjoy photographs being taken hence him not looking at the camera.

Photo: Col Walter W Ott

106. Sir Stafford Cripps (*centre*) on a visit to Burtonwood in 1943 with Colonel William H "Billy" Arnold (*left*) and General Ike Ott. Sir Stafford was Minister of Aircraft Production for the British Government with an obvious interest in Burtonwood.

Photo: Col Walter W Ott

107. *Top left:* Burtonwood was not just home to thousands of men during WWII but a large contingent of WACs arrived and mostly were billeted at Canada Hall, Padgate. This photo shows Corporal Evelyn (Vinnie) Lewis with Jerry Spignesi in 1944.

Photo: Vinnie Lewis

108. *Above:* Also taken at Canada Hall and with the typical living accommodation behind this photograph shows Corporal Vincent.

Photo: Vinnie Lewis

109. *Left:* WAC Stackey standing on the wheel of a P-51 Mustang long range fighter in 1944. The aircraft was named "Little Liz".

Photo: Vinnie Lewis

110. One of the many women who served with the WACs at Burtonwood during WWII. Mostly billeted on Canada Hall Site in Padgate, Warrington, they undertook many tasks in addition to secretarial and warehousing duties with some on Flight Test and many driving and doing similar duties. This shot is taken on Mary Ann Site adjacent to a C Type hangar with jeep, truck and crates piled up behind.

Photo: Carl J Winkleman

The Tasks

111. Every part of an aircraft was overhauled and proved to be in proper working condition before being passed to Flight Test. Here two armourers check guns from a B-17 on a mobile workbench.

Photo: Col Walter W Ott

112. Hundreds of freshly overhauled aero engines waiting to be delivered to USAAF stations throughout the UK, lined up outside building No 225 on Mary Ann Site; there was no room for all the engines under cover despite the constant building programme that continued for the whole of the war period. With an average of over 1,000 engines being produced per month it was a mammoth logistical job to physically move the volume of engines to their required bases. 30,386 engines were passed through BRD Site between 1 July 1943 and 5 May 1945.

Photo: Logan Muster

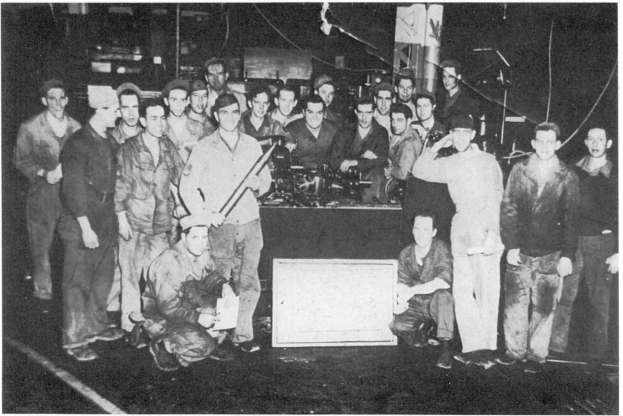

113. Maintenance Division celebrating the 1,000,000th part manufactured on BRD Site. The caption reads "1,000,000th PART MFG". The part is being held by the sergeant to the left of the sign.

Photo: Col Walter W Ott

114. Rows of benches in the Radio Repair Shop on BRD Site 1, 1945.

Photo: Col Walter W Ott

115. Furnaces and casts in the Propeller Shop on BRD Sites. Due to the difficulty in getting spares direct from the US, BAD1 set up its own production facility to supply anything that may be needed. 11,798 complete propeller assemblies were undertaken in WWII together with the manufacture of 18,171 prop blades.

Photo: Col Walter W Ott

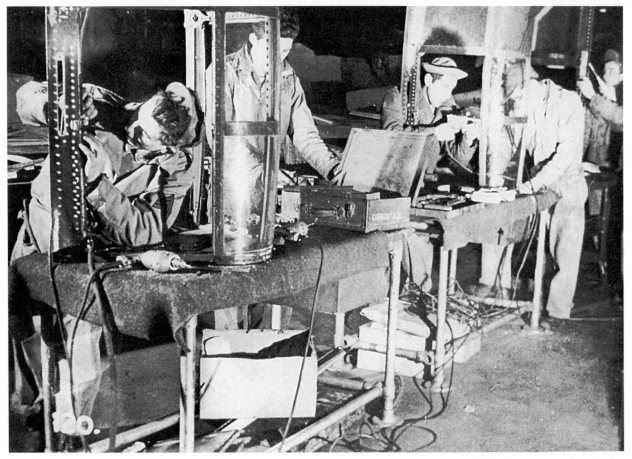

116. Men in the Canopy Shop on **BRD** Site assembling canopies on a production line basis.

Photo: Col Walter W Ott

117. Celebration in Engine Overhaul Division on completion of the record 2,048th engine in one month during August 1944. An all time record? No! It was beaten at Burtonwood in February 1945 with 2,155 engines produced in one month.

118. A close-up of an antenna installation on a C-47 probably named "Tricky Dicky". The workshops at Burtonwood worked with the scientists and designed mock ups and actual housings and aerials, and fitted the new radio and radar inventions onto aircraft for trials before putting them into quantity production once the best method was engineered. BAD1 manufactured thousands of kits for conversion and new installations, often in a very short time to meet operational requirements. This print is dated 2 October 1943.

Photo: via R M Armour

119. Close-up of prototype H2S equipment under the nose of B-17 "LaLLah V ...–" on E Site with the inside equipment covered from the photographer. Trials started in May 1943 and production for conversion of other aircraft was quickly put in hand.

Photo: via R M Armour

120. Technical design and Engineering section had no reference books so when they got single references or machinery handbooks they had to make up standards sheets, then printed copies to make up standards books for each man. This was the front page.

Photo: Carl J Winkleman

121. This CG-4A Glider was one of many received in crates by BAD1 for erection and delivery. The men of Maintenance Division received a request to experiment putting two engines onto one to see if it could be made to fly. T/Sgt Walter W Baerbalck and Carl Winkleman were two of the personnel to work on this project originating from Colonel William Arnold and passed down to Major McGee and then M/Sgt Mercer. With Lycoming 6 cylinder inverted engines begged from the British, the project ran for ninety days and was then abandoned. The crews requested that they be allowed to finish one and were granted permission with the final effort actually doing three hops over the base to prove its viability.

Photo: Milo Stites

122. A full frontal view of the CG-4A glider which was motorised by the men of Maintenance Division. Only one was finished due to the project being prematurely cancelled but it did fly on three or four occasions over the base as a testament to those who spent weeks designing and building modification kits so they could be manufactured by their hundreds if required.

Photo: Harry Holmes

123-125. This photograph and the two on the following page show the production line for modification and major overhaul of Republic F-84F Thunderstreaks on Mary Ann Site in 1954.

Photos: Ron Oldacre

Off Duty

Lester Moyer outside the American Red Cross Club in Southport which
the requisitioned Sunnyside Hotel. Originally this building was HQ
DA but it was taken over for other office duties in 1944. With the running
n of the main club in Southport at the Palace Hotel, Birkdale, the
nyside was taken over for the last few months of the war. Red Cross Clubs
d as bases for men away from their bases on leave or weekends with clubs
sited in Warrington, Liverpool and Manchester.

Photo: Lester Moyer

Newton C. B. & T. Club

Club Dance

Saturday, July 15, 1944

Newton C. B. & T. Club Band

Ticket 1/6.   Admission by Ticket only.

WELSHS

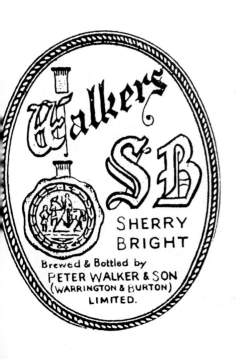

132. Eddie Kistler's *Swing Tips* all dressed up at the Palace Theatre in Warrington in 1944 doing a spoof of Kay Kayser's radio show College of Musical College. Eddie is standing in gown and mortar board to the right and Frank Otero is in the front row second from right in the sax section.

Photo: Frank Otero

133. In the early days Eddie Kistler's *Swing Tips* comprised *front row left to right:* Cros Rhodes, (singer); Peanuts Morris (sax); Glen Score (sax); Ed Brode (sax); Eddie Kistler (sax). *Second row:* Norman Locke; Jack Sweikert; James Brennan; Glen Score (guitar); Joe Baker (bass); Pop Huntington (piano) and Leo Navarette (drums).

Photo: Frank Otero

34. Eddie Kistler's *Swing Tips* Army Air Force Band at Burtonwood. Eddie (*standing left*) led the band for most of the war years and they played both on the base and at other centres like Canada Hall, Bruche Hall, the US Red Cross Clubs in Warrington, Liverpool and Manchester, ballrooms in all three towns and many other venues. At the end of the war they played with Vera Lynn and Ann Shelton at the London Palladium.

Photo: Walter W Ott

135. Glenn Miller and his band playing in one of his very last concerts on 15 August 1944. The band had played at Warton (BAD2) and flown to Burtonwood for another concert before flying to Bedford from where he set off on his last flight never to be seen again.

Photo: Vic Brown

 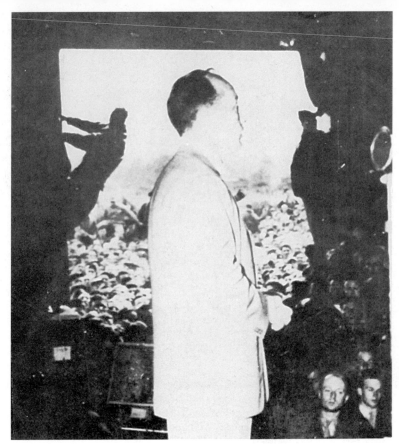

136-138. Bing Crosby at Burtonwood. *Above left:* The famous crooner pictured arriving at the base to entertain the troops in 1944. Many famous stars travelled across the Atlantic to England and they all passed through Burtonwood. *Above right:* Bing on stage. The stage was made of engine cases and Bing commented that it was probably the most valuable that he had ever worked off. Though Bing gave five or six shows during his 1944 visit, only one third of the men and women of BAD1 got to see him. *Below:* A youthful looking Bing Crosby with officers of BAD1 in 1944. The unknown lady is sitting on the lap of General 'Ike' Ott. Colonel William Arnold is behind, and to the right is Major W W 'Dewey' Ott.

139-141. Crosby's fellow *Road* star, Bob Hope, at Burtonwood in 1948. *Above left:* Hope has his first look at peace-time Burtonwood. *Above right:* On stage Bob and Delores Hope entertain the troops. The C type hangar on Mary Ann Site made an ideal auditorium but there were so many GI's at Burtonwood in the 40s and 50s that not everyone could get a seat. *Below:* Bob Hope and party. To the right of Hope are Father Kean and Delores; next to the RAF Commander is Colonel W W Ott, OC 59th Air Depot Wing.

Photos: Col Walter W Ott

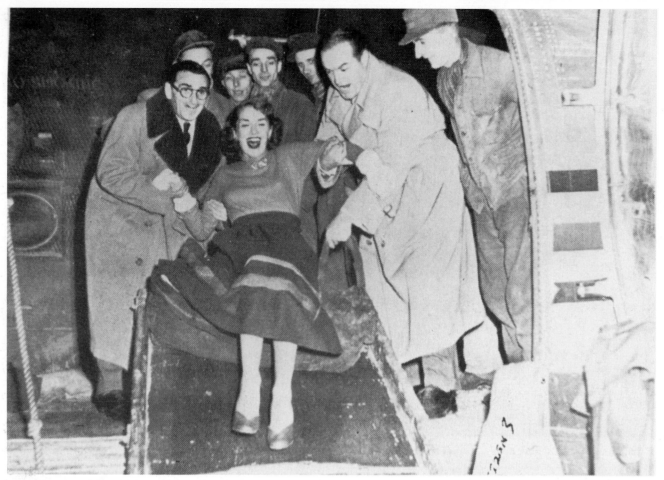

142-143. *Above:* Bob Hope and composer Irving Berlin 'help' star Jinx Falkenburgh out of a Berlin Airlift C-54. *Below:* Bob and Delores Hope with Jinx Falkenburgh and Father Kean are met by Colonel W W Ott at the base of the steps of a Douglas C-118A military transport, Burtonwood, 29 December 1948.

Photos: Col Walter W Ott

144-146. Flashback to the war years for a visit to Burtonwood by actor Jimmy Cagney. *Above left:* Cagney with Major W W 'Dewey' Ott and Colonel William H 'Billy' Arnold. *Above right:* Cagney surrounded by men of BAD1. The B-17 in the background has probably been named 'Doodle' in his honour after the song Yankee Doodle Dandy. *Below:* Cagney and fork lift truck driver on either Mary Ann or E Site.

147. Jean Simmons, the British film star, getting admiring looks from USAF Officers on a visit to Burtonwood on 15 December 1948. Leon Smith is 2nd from right.

Photo: Leon Smith

149. Brig General Troup Miller Jr, NAMA Command introduces Councillor Mary Hardman, Mayor of Warrington William Boyd also known as Hopalong Cassidy, one of the m famous cowboys on the US cinema and TV screen in the 19 Burtonwood, July 1953.

Photo: Burtonwood Bea

148. Famous singing star Nat "King" Cole entertains in the N Club, Burtonwood, circa 1953.

Photo: Burtonwood Bea

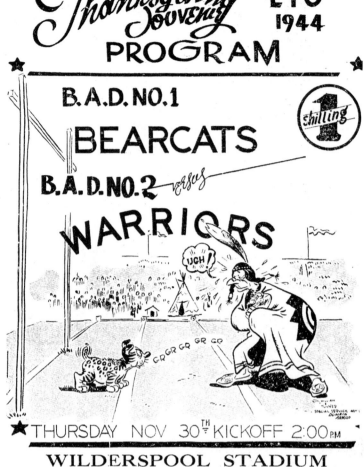

150. Sport was extremely popular with many teams being run by BAD1 and post-war units. The Burtonwood Bullets football team played all over the UK and Europe with a very high success rate. Here is one of the baseball pitches on No 2 Site in 1944.

Photo: Foster F Martin

151. *Right:* Thanksgiving Day, 30 November 1944, was celebrated by a football match between the BAD1 Bearcats from Burtonwood and the BAD2 Warriors from Warton. The Warriors won 24-0.

152. *Below:* A baseball match in progress on the main sports site to the side of Site 2 in 1944.

Photo: Foster F Martin

Aircraft

153. A-35B Vultee Vengeance two seat dive bombers lined up outsid[e]
Mary Ann Site in 1943. The original "Fort" type control tower ca[n]
be seen in the background. It was demolished to make way for th[e]
hardstandings outside Mary Ann Site when the new 12779/41 towe[r]
was built. Vengeances were conceived as dive bombers but many we[re]
converted to act as target tugs. Used by the USAAF and the RA[F]
these aircraft were powered by a Wright R-2600-13 radial engine an[d]
could reach a top speed of 279 mph and had a range of 550 miles.
Photo: Arthur L Smit[h]

154. *Below:* A B-24 Liberator four engined bomber stripped down fo[r]
inspection of the production line at Burtonwood in 1944. The hanga[r]
is a C type depicting that it is on Mary Ann Site in either hangar 3, [4]
or 5. BAD1 produced 694 B-24's between 1 July 1943 and 8 May 1945[.]
Photo: Col Walter W O[tt]

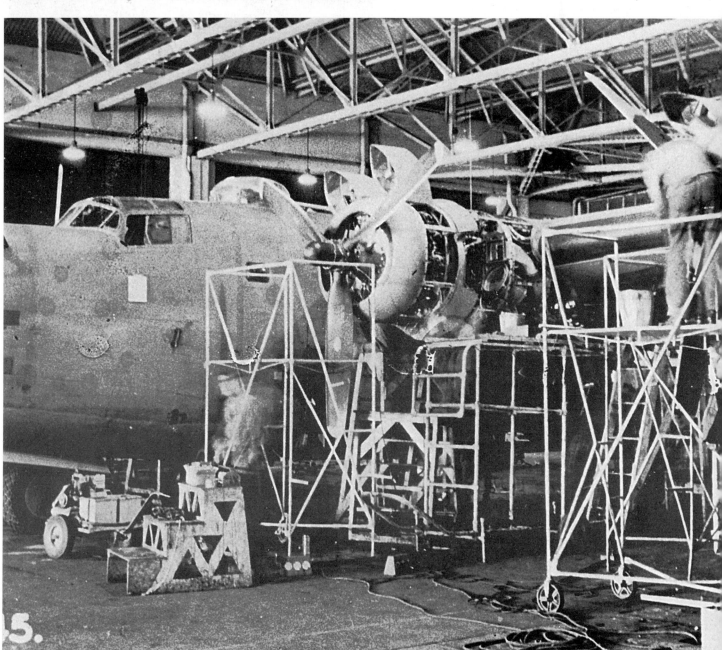

5.

155. P-38 Lightning twin engined fighters being assembled after delivery across the Atlantic by ship to Liverpool docks. The aircraft would be assembled, minutely checked, test flown and then delivered to their front line squadrons. Between 1 July 1943 and 8 May 1945 4,381 P-47's were produced by BAD1.

Photo: Col Walter W Ott

156. Newly delivered B-17s lined up on the taxiway at Burtonwood ready to go through the production hangars. The airman and jeep in the foreground give scale to the size of the aircraft. The main aircraft featured is serialed 338154. BAD1 produced 4,243 B-17s in the period 1 July 1943 to 5 May 1945 and it was not unknown for up to fifty to arrive in a single day. Generally throughout the war at least four hangars were working on B-17s on a production line basis 24 hours a day every day of the year.

Photo: Col Walter W Ott

157-158. Boeing B-17 337716 was the 5,000th aircraft to be processed by BAD1 in WWII. The honour fell to a hangar on Mary Ann Site in 1944. Everyone who worked on the aircraft wrote their names on it and it was christened "5 Grand". BAD1 went on to produce 4,243 B-17s alone and a grand total of 11,575 aircraft in WWII.

Photo: Col Walter W Ott

159. A B-17 undergoing maintenance on either Tech or A Sites. The cowlings have been removed from the Wright Cyclone R-1820 engines for inspection.

Photo: via Col Walter W Ott

160. Another evocative shot of the 1944 flight line with a B-17 in the foreground with different coloured engine cowlings surrounded by similar types with the exception of the B-26 Marauder alongside. Note the clear, slightly cloudy sky and deep shadows. All the fuss about the permanent bad weather is proved to be untrue!

Photo: Carl J Winkleman

161. Busy scene inside a J Type hangar on Tech Site in 1944. In the foreground is B-17 Fortress *Luscious* serial 25725 which even has its engines named with *Phyllis* and *Scottie* on starboard outer and inner respectively. Another B-17 serialled 237981 can be seen in the background and there is a B-24 facing the hangar door in the background. These aircraft are obviously not new and therefore were returned to BAD1 for either conversion or modification. The positioning shows that they were slightly twisted off the hangar centre-line to pack as many as possible into each hangar.

162. A tranquil scene on the edge of Burtonwood's dispersals in 1944. The cows graze ignorant of the lethal packages parked alongside them. These B-17s are all new with 339164 in the centre. Every available inch of parking space was taken up as the Maintenance and Supply Divisions worked 24 hours every day to keep the supply of aircraft flowing to the squadrons. The average time aircraft stayed at Burtonwood was often no more than seven days.

Photo: Col Walter W Ott

163. Another posed shot for the official photographer in 1944, this shows men at work on another B-17 on A Site. During 1944 and 1945 it was not unusual to have over 350 of these aircraft on the ground at any one time and over fifty would be delivered in and out per week to keep up with demand.

Photo: Col Walter W Ott

164. B-24 Liberators in a hangar on Mary Ann Site forming part of the Carpetbagger programme. This involved aircraft being converted for clandestine operations over occupied Europe dropping agents and supplies to the resistance movements. The aircraft were painted overall black and had their armament removed to make them faster. The shiny black underside can be seen on the aircraft to the right and the turret has been removed from the rear aircraft.

Photo: via Col Walter W Ott

165. A B-24 Liberator named *Wee Wass* being towed onto PSP (pierced steel planking) in one of the dispersals. Note the white helmeted policeman on the right acting as guard. This is one of 694 Liberators processed through Burtonwood with the majority being processed at BAD2 Warton.

An everyday sight on the flight line at Burtonwood in ...-45. The B-24 Liberator serial 2528 dominates the ground but is surrounded by other types including a ... and oddly painted B-17 to the left with a white fin ...rudder with a P-47 just behind. To the right can be ... the white fin of another C-47 and two P-47 ...nderbolts.

Photo: Carl J Winkleman

167. The sleek lines of the Martin B-26 Marauder can be seen here, this one with its unusual bomb bay doors in the open position. 444 Marauders were produced by BAD1 together with thousands of its Pratt & Whitney R-2800 radial engines. The Marauder had a maximum speed of 317 mph and could carry a bomb load of 4,000 lbs with a normal range of 1,150 miles.

...8. A Veteran B-26 Marauder twin engined bomber ...led WT-B about to be moved by tug on BRD Site 1944.
Photo: Carl J Winkleman

169. Although only a limited number of Marauders were produced at Burtonwood, several hundred were scrapped here after hostilities ceased. Here a line up of war-weary B-26s can be seen, with a P-38 Lightning in the foreground awaiting scrapping.

Photo: George Heid

170. A fine shot of another Martin B-26 Marauder with the hangars of Tech Site behind.

Photo: via Harry Holmes

NO SMOKING

171. A Piper L-4 Grasshopper being uncrated and readied for flight on BRD Site. These aircraft were used for observation and liaison, had two seats and a 65 hp inline Continental engine giving a maximum speed of 88 mph and a loaded weight of 1,160 lb. It is clearly one of the smallest aircraft to operate out of Burtonwood. A total of over 158 L-1, L-4 and L-5s were processed by BAD.

Photo: via Col Walter W

172-173. Several C-47 Dakotas were modified in the BAD1 shops for use by generals in the field. They became HQ and home to the commanding Generals in the invasion of Europe and these two photographs show the fine workmanship that went into making these transport aircraft usable as a mobile home including sitting room, bedroom, shower and toilet. Telephone and bed light can be seen by the bunk in the bedroom.

Photos: Howard Polesky

174. Typical photograph illustrating the work in BRD Site. In the background are two P-38 Lightnings, the one to the left still in its protective cosmoline coating after the voyage across the Atlantic on board ship. They were assembled and modified on this site and towed across to Flight Test for a test "hop" prior to delivery to the active squadrons. In the foreground can be seen the dismantled engines undergoing overhaul.

Photo: via Col Walter W Ott

175. Inside a hangar on either A or Tech Sites these P-38 Lightnings are receiving their final touches on the production line prior to being passed over to Flight Test for their test hops. Powered by two 1,150 hp Allison engines these fighters could reach a top speed of 357 mph and a height of 40,000 ft. A total of 1,004 were processed by BAD1 in two years. Eleven can be seen in this hangar.

Photo: via Col Walter W Ott

176. War-weary P-38 Lightnings lined up at Burtonwood dispersal in 1945.

Photo: Harry Holmes

177. P-47 Thunderbolts in a hangar on Mary Ann Site (either AD4, 5 or 6) undergoing complete overhaul comprising testing every part and usually providing a replacement engine. The original engine would go to the BRD Site for overhaul and be put in store for the next aircraft delivery or sent to the active fighter stations for replacement when needed. Thousands of engines were dispatched by road or rail all over the UK and, after the invasion of France, also to Europe. An R-2800 Double-Wasp engine can be seen in the left foreground.

Photo: via Col Walter W Ott

178. Line up of P-47 Thunderbolts on one of the dispersals at Burtonwood in 1944. The one in the foreground is serialled 16368. The obstructed canopy of the earlier models such as this were replaced by clear canopies made at Burtonwood.

179. Technicians working on a R-2800 Double-Wasp radial engine on a P-47D Thunderbolt. This engine delivered 2,300 hp and gave the Thunderbolt a maximum top speed of 426 mph. This engine was by far the most common at Burtonwood with literally thousands being processed through BRD Site on a production line basis.

Photo: via Col Walter W Ott

180. A further line up of P-47 Thunderbo[l]
awaiting to be called to the hangars for attenti[on]
in 1944.

Photo: George Heide[r]

181. A May or June day at Burtonwood with the
sun shining on this P-47 Thunderbolt serial
227249 resplendent in invasion markings ready
for work on the Normandy beaches. A P-38
Lightning can be seen behind with another
invasion marked P-47 facing the camera. The slag
heap at the nearby coal mine can be seen in the
distance and it was this one that a B-24 crashed
into during 1944 on its take-off on return to the
States with all on board being killed.

Photo: via Col Walter W Ott

182. P-61 Northrop Black Widows lined up o[n]
Site in 1944. The one nearest the camera [is]
serialled 239739. Powered by two Twin Wa[sp]
radial engines this aircraft was a night fighter a[nd]
usually found in this black colour scheme. [They]
were processed by BAD1 between July 1943 a[nd]
May 1945. Several were converted for clandest[ine]
"Carpetbagger" operations. The sign in [the]
background reads "Supply Division – 1st BA[D"]
but the rest is indecipherable. Note the canvas [on]
the hangar door behind to break up the line in [the]
event of enemy recce or attack, and the slipp[ery]
grass spread over the curved roof of this Lame[lla]
type hangar.

Photo: Carl J Winkle[r]

183-184. Two of a series of many photographs taken in June 1944 showing aircraft just unloaded from ships in Liverpool docks being taken to Burtonwood for re-erection, modification, test flight and delivery. The first shows four P-47 Thunderbolts being escorted across the Pier Head at Liverpool with the police clearing the way. A preferred route was determined for the wide roads with no obstructions to ensure that the oversized loads did not receive or cause any damage. The rudders and elevators have been removed as have the propellers. With the balance of weight off centre due to the engine's weight, special racks were made on the US vehicles to transport them. Many P-47s also went to Speke Airport to the Lockheed facility which also erected them prior to delivery.

Photos: Flight

185-186. Two more from the same series show P-51 Mustangs being towed to Speke Airport where the Lockheed Corporation undertook erection and then flew them to Warton (BAD2) for final mods, test hop and delivery.

Photos: Flight

187. A row of Vultee Vengeances with wings folded being towed to Burtonwood behind an old Vauxhall police car. Note that these aircraft are already carrying RAF markings. Taken on 22 June 1944.

Photo: Flight

188. An interesting line up of aircraft in 1944. *Left to right:* a P-47 Thunderbolt, North American AT-6 Texan, Noorduyn UC-64 Norseman and Douglas C-47 Dakota.

Photo: Carl J Winkleman

189. A Messerschmit Me108, four seater communications aircraft captured from the Germans is inspected on Mary Ann Site in 1945. This low wing monoplane was developed before the war and constructed in both Germany and France. The development was useful in the design of the German's premier fighter, the Me109, which followed the general arrangement of this type. The RAF also captured three of these aircraft and named them Aldons, the authors namesake!

190. A C-47 Dakota belonging to Northern Air Materiel Area (NAMA), the resident unit at Burtonwood from September 1953 to June 1958.
Photo: Roger Bate

191. Another study of a common sight – a C-47 Dakota on the pan outside Mary Ann Site with Tech Site behind.

Photo: Roger Bate

A Lockheed C-121 (Constellation) parked on Tech Site ramp in 1955 with hangar "J" in the background. Used for transport of passengers and freight this aircraft could handle sixty passengers or a 40,000 lb cargo payload over a range of approximately 4,600 miles. The sign on the hangar door reads: "Airfreight Terminal, 6th Aerial Port Squadron".

Photo: Ron Oldacre

193. Never based here, this Boeing B-47 Stratojet is on a visit for the Open House on 18 May 1957 and is seen lined up outside Mary Ann Site adjacent to KC-97G Stratofreighter 22678 and a WB-50 of the 53rd Weather Recon Sqn.

Photo: Roger Bate

194. The nose of KC-97G 22678 at the 1957 Open House. The military version of the Stratocruiser this aircraft had four 3,500 hp Pratt & Whitney R-4360-59 engines giving it a range of 4,200 miles and a cruising speed of 300 mph. Fully loaded this aircraft weighed in at 153,000 lbs. Note the white painted area around the flight deck to reflect the sun.

Photo: Ron Oldacre

195. A Douglas C-118 131616 newly arrived f[...] the States at rest on the Tech Site pan in 1[...] Utilised by MATS, this military version of [...] Douglas DC-6 was the main passenger airc[...] linking the US with Europe via Burtonwood [...] many years in the 1950s. In its cargo role it co[...] carry 28,500 lbs of freight in 5,000 cu f[...] unobstructed cargo space. In its passenger ro[...] could carry 76 fully equipped troops across [...] Atlantic at a speed of 316 mph at a crui[...] altitude of 23,100 ft.

Photo: Roger [...]

196. Another view of the same aircraft showing the MATS steps inscribed with 1602nd Support Squadron (H) Burtonwood.

Photo: Roger Bate

197. A close-up of a visiting C-118 with the WW[...] control tower in the background.

Photo: Ron Olda[...]

198. A North American F-86E Sabre undergoing a Major overhaul at Mary Ann Site in 1956. This illustrates Burtonwood's role as major maintenance for the USAF in Britain being capable of undertaking third and fourth line servicing without the necessity of ferrying aircraft back to the States for major work.

Photo: Ron Oldacre

199. A North American F-86D Sabre on the ramp on Mary Ann Site. This was one of the mainstays of the USAF fighter force in the 1950s and was capable of 715 mph and a service ceiling of 45,000 ft. It was powered by one General Electric J47-GE-17 engine.

Photo: Roger Bate

200. An F-86 Sabre being unloaded from a C-124 Globemaster on the ramp after a flight from Italy. It came to Burtonwood for major overhaul and rework prior to returning to its unit in Italy.

201. A Republic F-84 in a C Type hangar on Mary Ann Site undergoing modification work in 1956.

Photo: Ron Oldacre

202. Republic F-84F Thunderstreak on display at the Open House on 17 May 1957.

Photo: Phil H Butler

203. A Fairchild C-123B Provider at Burtonwood Open House, 18 May 1957. This aircraft was one of many of this type maintained in the overhaul facility (NAMA) at Burtonwood.

Photo: Phil H Butler

. A very common C-124 Globemaster on the
h Site ramp in the 1950s with its front loading/
oading doors open to unload another load
ught across the Atlantic from the US. Able to
ry passengers in the upper fuselage and cargo
he lower part, it could hold a maximum of 200
ops for a range of 6,280 miles.

Photo: Roger Bate

205. A fine shot of C-124 No 21065 on runway 09
in 1957 with undercarriage and flaps down. Note
the small radar housing in the nose.

Photo: Roger Bate

6. NAMA Burtonwood based T-33 Shooting
ar two seat trainer on the ramp in 1957.
obably used by the Commanding Officer for
mmunications duties and by test pilots for
ntinuation training, this aircraft was the stan-
rd USAF advanced trainer for many years and
uld reach a speed of 580 mph with a range of
45 miles. It could be fitted with two 0.5 in M-3
achine guns.

Photo: Ron Oldacre

207-208. A Convair B-36 Peacemaker heavy bomber about to touch down on runway 09 in 1956. Although never actually based for any time here these giant bombers visited several times for short stays to familiarise both the crews and ground personnel with their operation here. The runway was extended in 1953 to be long enough to handle any aircraft then flying and the B-36 required the longest run. Even at 9,000 feet long the runway (09-27) was not considered long enough for this aircraft to safely take-off fully loaded. The aircraft was powered by six 3,800 hp Pratt & Whitney R-4360-41 piston engines mounted in the "pusher" position behind the wings, plus four 5,200 lb st General Electric J-47-GE-19 jet engines outboard for assistance on take-off and "over target boost". Maximum speed was 436 mph but cruising speed was only 290 mph. This monster had a range of 10,000 miles, a maximum weight of 408,000 lbs, a span of 230 ft, length of 162 ft and a height to the top of the fin of 46 ft 9 ins. The last of 380 B-36s was delivered to the USAF on August 14, 1954. Designed to fly faster and higher than any current fighter, it was outmoded almost as soon as it entered service as fighter development overtook the development programme of this aircraft.　　　Photos: Roger Bate

210. An SA-16 Albatross of C Flight, 9th Air Rescue Squadron based at Burtonwood from 1 July 1951 until 14 November 1952, when it was replaced by 68th Air Rescue Squadron which stayed until 18 November 1953 when it moved north to Prestwick. The unit was primarily tasked with rescue of US service aircrew but also took part in many civilian rescues.

Photo: Burtonwood Beacon

209. Engineers working on a B-36 in the open as they could not fit into the hangars. Note the size of the open bomb bay door under the aircraft.

Photo: Ron Oldacre

211. Two giant B-36s at rest with the sun going down between their wings.

Photo: Ron Oldacre

212. An early C-130 Hercules unloading at Burtonwood after a trans-Atlantic flight. Several Burtonwood personnel travelled to the States to learn how to handle these new aircraft but the military terminal moved to Mildenhall before they came into quantity production and few were to be seen gracing the ramp at Burtonwood.   Photo: Ron Oldacre

213. De Havilland LH-20A Beaver at Burtonwood Open House on 17 May 1958. This aircraft was Burtonwood based with NAMA.

Photo: Phil H Butler

4. The last fixed-wing aircraft to be based at Burtonwood were the gliders of No 631 Gliding School operated by Air Cadets for the giving of air experience to cadets and for training them up to solo standard, and in some cases beyond. Here the gliders are seen in one of the J type hangars on Tech Site which was their home for many years.

Photo: Bryan Trunkfield

215. A Slingsby T.31B Cadet TX3 over the hangars and storage warehouses on G Site to the rear of No 6 Site. The concrete bases of some of the nissen huts can be seen immediately behind the hangars with the curved L type hangars on the left and the airfield top right. Photo taken approximately 1970.

Photo: Bryan Trunkfield

6. WE991 a Slingsby T.30B Prefect TX1 single seater der of 631 Gliding School seen over the western end of away 09 with the nissen huts of Lythgoe Site (No 6 Site) the foreground.

Photo: Bryan Trunkfield

217. A montage of photographs put together by the base photo lab showing a small cross section of the nose-art seen at Burtonwood on aircraft returning for repairs or modifications. Included is Buggs Bunny "Hare's to ya", Donald Duck "Betta Duck", and some star signs "Leo" although this one is accidentally reversed! Others include the usual girls, "Booby Trap", "Paper Doll", "Broadway Rose", "Heavenly Body" and "Quitcherbitchen-Elsie".

Photo: Bill Thomas

218. Satan's Daughter is another example of ladies adorning the sides of bombers to remind the guys of the girls back home.

Photo: Joe Meyerson

220. "Sleepy Time Gal" at rest in a Burtonwood dispersal in 1945 comprising a B-24 Liberator with covers over its nose turret. Photo: James M Albers

0. Lt Tusett alongside P-38J Lightning "Happy Jack's Go ggy" claiming eight Luftwaffe aircraft and two trains. Note aircraft standing on a PSP hardstanding in a dispersal. Photo: Frank Zeller

221. Not restricted to fighter and bomber aircraft this C-47 has a graphically illustrated piece of art-work depicting its transport role. BAD1 March 1945. Photo: Joe Meyerson

3. Chattanooga Choo Choo, alias a B-24 Liberator owing its impressive score.

Photo: James M Albers Jr

2. *Right:* B-24 Strange Cargo? gets an admiring look in 45. The note in brackets states it was crewed by "9 men and oy" Photo: James M Albers Jr

Berlin
Airlift

224. Men of the 59th Air Depot Wing arriving at the Princes Landing Stage in Liverpool on 12 September 1948 to re-open Burtonwood after two years back in RAF control. Shortly after they had settled down not only were they undertaking 200 hour overhauls on C-54s but three fully equipped B-29 bomb groups, consisting of 90 aircraft, had settled down at four bases in eastern England for what was officially described as "routine training" missions. Two of these groups had been moved to the UK from Germany whilst the third had flown in from the States.

Photo: Burtonwood Beacon

225. Busy hangar scene on Mary Ann Site showing three of the C-54s undergoing their 200 hour overhaul prior to returning to the Berlin Airlift. The overhaul was organised on a production line basis starting with the removal of all loose equipment for checking, followed by a complete clean both internally and externally before being passed on for engine and systems checks. By February 1949 seven C-54s were delivered in one 24 hour period but by March eleven were delivered in one day with a total of 83 returning to Germany in A1 condition in the first 15 days of March.

Photo: Wayne Jordan

226. Lost in the reflection on the side of this Douglas C-54 Skymaster is the caption "1,000th Aircraft Through Burtonwood" meaning the 1,000th aircraft in the Berlin Airlift to be processed through for its 200 hour overhaul. The Russians started the Berlin Blockade in June 1948 and the British and US Governments set up an airlift named Operation Vittles by the USAF. The C-54 was the standard USAF transport and the maximum number was pressed into service to supply Berlin with everything from the air to sustain normal life. Newly re-opened Burtonwood started to accept aircraft in October 1948 when 59th Air Depot Wing was set up to undertake the work.

227-228. Men of 59th Air Depot Group working on another C-54 on Mary Ann Site. This section of the work is known as Station No 3 and the work includes Engines, Instruments, Electrical, Sheet metal and Fuel cells. Prior to this stage it had been stripped of all loose equipment and then cleaned thoroughly. Here the engine cowlings have been removed for a physical check or replacement subject to each engine's individual hours run since the last change. During the Berlin Blockade the men of Burtonwood worked a 24 hour, three shift day to ensure that the aircraft were on the ground for the shortest possible time.

Photo: Wayne Jorda

229. Totally surrounded by purpose-built timber docks in hangar J on Tech Site another C-54 Skymaster is checked before returning to Germany and the Airlift. These aircraft carried everything from coal to flour, razor blades and soap powder and the inevitable spillage caused considerable problems for the cleaning crews who had to clean them thoroughly even throughout the cold winter of 1948-49. 309 C-54 s were employed together with R-5Ds, C-82s and C-47s with most C-54s making several visits to Burtonwood between October 1948 and May 1949. Total American costs were estimated at $346,698,500 in 1949 values!!

230. The worst job on the aircraft from Operation Vittles was cleaning them and it was even worse in winter when the men were still using cold water. A hangar on A Site was set up as a cleaning section to allow the work to continue day and night regardless of whether it was freezing outside or not. This photograph depicts the muck and grime being cleaned out of another C-54 Skymaster immediately after its arrival at Burtonwood.

Photo: Wayne Jorda

FIRST BERLIN AIRLIFT CRAFT TO GET MAINTENANCE HERE

231. The men of the 59th Air Depot Wing who worked on the first Skymaster aircraft about to be returned to the Airlift in late 1948.

Photo: Burtonwood Beacon

232. October 1948 saw the first C-54 Skymaster to pass through Burtonwood and here are the men that worked on it on a cold, wet day, ready to send it back to duty in Germany. Conditions at Burtonwood were terrible with the men re-occupying huts that had been empty for two years and had leaks, draughts, little heat and which were in a sea of mud miles from the mess hall and recreation areas. After a few months every considerable effort was made to improve living conditions.

ARRIVAL 1ST 2ND 3RD 4TH 5TH 6TH ROTATION

---after six, long, grueling, backbreaking months on the Airlift, you were rotated
back to your home base where you wished you were back flying the Airlift again, and some of you were---

---it was an easy guess as to who flew in the coal
and who flew in the flour---

---the Combined Airlift Task Force ran
smoothly, but we did have our little differences---

---you thought Geisla was calling but it turned out
to be the Ops Officer telling you that your plane
was leaving in ten minutes---

---Operation Santa Claus, when ol' Saint Nick brought
all those Christmas presents to the kids of Berlin
in his four-engined reindeer---

234. Close-up of the nose of a WB-50 of the 53rd Weather Recon Squadron at the 1956 Open House. Note the crew's name on the nose. This is a derivative of the B-29 Superfortress which saw action in the Pacific in the closing months of WWII.

Photo: Roger Bate

235. The C type hangar of Mary Ann Site was home to the WB-50s from 1953 to 1959. Only two or three could fit in the hangar at a time due to their length of 99 ft and wing span of 141 ft 3 in. One aircraft would take off each morning on Falcon mission, a data gathering flight across the western part of the Atlantic for weather forecasting.

Photo: Ron Oldacre

236. The tails of WB-50s 90288 and 90275 of the 53rd Weather Recon Squadron in 1956. One aircraft would average 2,700 miles each day on set routes and fixed altitudes to take specific weather recordings. Each flight would last fifteen hours with some flights being as long as 3,600 miles, mostly over water without navigational aids. There were two routine routes – Falcon Alfa and Falcon Bravo – with a third – Falcon Coca – routing to Saudi Arabia occasionally flown. Each flight would have a ten man crew.

Photo: Ron Oldacre

237-238. The essential maintenance being carried out on one of the four Pratt & Whitney R-4360-35 engines on a WB-50.

Photo: Roger Bate

239. A Boeing WB-50D Superfortress of the 53rd Weather Reconnaissance Squadron on display at the Open Day in May 1957.

Photo: Phil H Butler

240. Maintenance men on a WB-50 on the pan on Mary Ann Site with several other aircraft of 53rd Weather Recon Sqn in the background, 1957.

Photo: Donald Squib

Accidents

241-244. Many USAAF aircraft force landed in Switzerland during the war and were interned. After the fall of Germany a select band of engineers from BAD1, Burtonwood, flew out to return them to the UK wherever possible. Here a B-17 beyond repair is cut in half after its engines were removed and flipped onto its back so the undercarriage can be removed and parts used to repair another. James Albers is seen on the wing cutting free the landing gear with a Swiss mechanic. Another shot shows two B-24 Liberators well beyond repair awaiting scrapping. All photographs at Dubendorf in 1945.

Photos: James M Albers

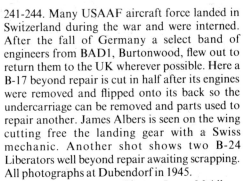

245-246. This C-47 Dakota was lucky to escape blowing up when it became entangled with a fuel bowser whilst taxiing in the early 1950s.

Photos: Ron Oldacre

247-248. Two photographs of a North American B-45 Tornado which came to grief after an undercarriage collapse on landing at Burtonwood in 1953. This light bomber and photo reconnaissance aircraft had a top speed of 550 mph and was powered by four 5,200 lb static thrust General Electric J47-GE-15 turbojets giving it a bomb load of 20,000 lbs. It was obsolete by 1955.

Photos: Ron Oldacre

249-252. WB-29 Superfortress of 53rd Weat
Reconnaissance Squadron which developed eng
trouble whilst over Greenland 1,300 miles from home
10,000 ft No 3 fuel tank booster became inoperative a
the aircraft turned back descending to 9,000 ft to conse
fuel and give optimum performance. It covered 1,
miles to Prestwick but because of communicat
difficulty an instrument approach was impossible so
pilot opted to try to return to Burtonwood. Forty m
south of Prestwick No 1 engine had to be closed down,
2 developed similar fuel flow difficulties and No 4 g
indications of the same thing happening. At 23.30
order to abandon the aircraft was given with all ele
parachuting to safety. The aircraft had been pointed
to sea but after the pilot had jumped it turned and cras
at Lupton Fell near Keswick on the edge of the L
District.

The photographs show an aerial view of the crash site w
the tail more or less intact, close ups of the tail section a
the remains of one of the engines.

Photos: Ron Olda

253-254. A "nearly" accident when C-118 272673 approached with the nose wheel jammed pointing right. After a slow approach and very gentle touch down the pilot held the nose off the ground for as long as possible before it touched the runway. Fortunately for all on board, it immediately freed itself and became steerable, thus saving the aircraft veering off the runway. These shots show it after it had just touched down, the fire trucks surrounding it just in case and the relieved crew and passengers climbing out where it stopped on the runway.

Photos: Ron Oldacre

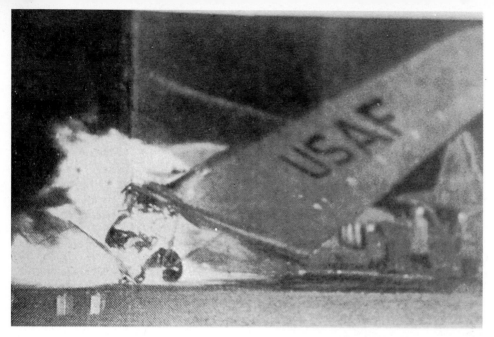

255. The burning hulk of a C-47 at the end
runway 09 on 4 January 1952. A US Navy P
Lockheed Neptune had departed fr
Burtonwood for Keflavik, Iceland but had
return due to bad weather. Weather
Burtonwood was also very bad and it landed sl
of the runway (which had not yet been lengthen
and broke up. The nose section bounced and
the C-47 which was warming up ready for take
The C-47 caught fire and was burned out. Six w
killed but 18 survived although some had seri
burns. Fortunately this was the last recorded fa
accident at Burtonwood and there were ma
thousands of aircraft movements to follow c
the next eight years.

Photo: Burtonwood Bea

256. A Kirkby Cadet Mk III glider with a very
crumpled wing after attacking a fence on Mary
Ann Site in about 1969. No 631 Gliding School
was at Burtonwood from November 1959 until
September 1983 when the demolition and taking
up of runways prevented successful gliding
operations. Thousands of local Air Cadets had
their first experience of gliding here and hundreds
gained their gliding certificates at Burtonwood
soaring above the once proud base.

Photo: Bryan Trunkfield

257. This unidentified Norse Norseman flip
onto its back whilst landing at Burtonwood i
strong cross-wind in 1944.

Photo: Thomas E Cor

Scrap

The end of the war saw an immediate change
... from production to scrapping. Here on
... Site in 1945 aircraft were sometimes taken
... packing cases and scrapped there and then.
... known as "Salvage" hundreds of aircraft
... their days under the scrapman's axe at
... onwood.

Photo: Carl J Winkleman

259. After being worked on for three months on
BRD Site this P-61 Black Widow night fighter is
being ripped to shreds as surplus to requirements
on BRD Site in 1945. Many of these aircraft were
delivered to BAD1 but never flown out as they
arrived too late to take part in the conflict and it
was not worth while to return them to the US as
there were surplus airframes already littering that
country.

Photo: J E Humphreys

... Unfortunately many aircraft were beyond
... overy and were cannibalised to recover spares
... se on other aircraft. Here a B-17 has been cut
... wo: two steel cables are attached to the back of
... cks with loops passing over the fuselage and, by
... ving away, they cut the aircraft in two like a
... ese cutter.

Photo: James M Albers

Other Visitors

261. October 1950 saw Field Marshal Sir Bernard Montgomery "Monty" visit Burtonwood, seen here with Brig General Robert C Oliver, 59th Air Depot Wing Commander.

Photo: Burtonwood Beacon

262. *Below:* In March 1953 HRH The Duke of Edinburgh visited Burtonwood and saluted the colours with Brig General Robert C Oliver, Commander. Over 10,000 Americans saw the Duke including USAF personnel and dependents.

Photo: Burtonwood Beacon

263. *Below right:* With bible in hand evangelist Billy Graham preaches at Burtonwood on 11 May 1954. On his trip to the UK he also visited USAF bases at Wethersfield, Molesworth and Brize Norton.

Photo: Burtonwood Beacon

Vickers Valiant B(PR)K.1 WZ 405 of 207 [Squa]dron RAF based at Marham visited to form [part] of the static display for the 18 May 1957 Open [Hou]se. Valiants, Victors and Vulcans were [oper]ated at Burtonwood from the operational [read]iness platform at the end of runway 09 for [man]y years after the USAF gave up the airfield. It [was] used as a scatter airfield to be brought into use [by V]-Bombers in the event of the threat of war to [sprea]d our bombing resources around all airfields [with] runways long and strong enough to [with]stand fully loaded bombers.

Photo: Roger Bate

265. Gloster Javelin XA631 all weather fighter of No 23 Squadron from RAF Coltishall, Norfolk, visiting as part of the RAF element of the 17 May 1958 Open House.

Photo: Roger Bate

Hunter F6 XF527 of 19 Squadron based at [Chu]rch Fenton in Yorkshire forming part of the [H]ome static display in May 1958.

Photo: Roger Bate

47TH AREA
SUPPORT GROUP

U.S. ARMY
RESERVE STORAGE ACTIVITY
RAF BURTONWOOD

267. Always an RAF Station, Burtonwood only received its own badge in 1989 thanks to the work of Squadron Leader John Tisbury the RAF Commander. The badge is based on the Support Command badge but is personal to Burtonwood.

268. The current sign at the main entrance to the US Army fac Burtonwood comprising Site 8, also known as the Header l Constructed in 1953-4 this building was, and may still be, the larges warehouse in Europe. The US Army also occupies Site 3 which is now a site with residential bungalows.

Photo: Aldon P Fe

270-271. Two examples of aviation art in the form of murals were fo a hangar on A Site during the Burtonwood Association's Reunion i The aircraft is a B-17 Fortress the like of which filled the hangar and for three wartime years. Its last three numbers were 402 so it must ha modelled on an actual aircraft. The writing under the aircraft say Smoking". The other shows the badge of Air Service Command U which controlled the base for much of WWII.

Photos: Aldon P Fe

269. Tail of C-47 0-348809 sporting the NAMA Europe badge on the tail, resident at Burtonwood on 18 May 1957.

Photo: Roger Bate

Demolition

The sign says it all. Now owned by the War-ton and Runcorn Development Corporation, airfield site had been allowed to deteriorate so ...ch that there was no alternative but to tear it ...wn and redevelop the site. However, the work ...menced in 1986 and by summer 1989 it was ... not completed which is a statement on the size ... scale of the base and the strength with which ...se "Temporary" wartime buildings were ...structed. Like a great giant slowly dying it was ...ctant to let go. Obviously some locals were ... distressed to see the demolition as there are ... lumps of earth on the top of the sign board ...iously thrown by someone!

Photo: Aldon P Ferguson

273. The sad sight of the demolition of a C Type hangar on Mary Ann Site in June 1986. During WWII this was hangar AD-5 responsible for the production of hundreds of P-38s, P-47s, B-17s and B-24s and subsequently saw service undertaking 200 hour overhauls for C-54s on the Berlin Airlift. It was then the servicing hangar for WB-29s and WB-50s of the 53rd Weather Recon Sqn and mods to all contemporary 1950s USAF aircraft.

Photo: Aldon P Ferguson

...4. Big holes were cut into this J Type hangar on ...ch Site before it was literally cut down and cut ... for scrap. The new control tower can just be ...n to the left of the hangar. This hangar was ...d by Flight Test during WWII and saw every ...e of WWII USAAF aircraft inside. It was last ...d by the gliders of No 631 Gliding School. The ...oto was taken on 24 August 1987.

Photo: Aldon P Ferguson

275. The end of one of the three L type hangars G Site in September 1986.

Photo: Aldon P Fergu

276. The destruction of the HQ buildings at the main entrance to Tech Site. These buildings formed part of the original RAF main site and were eventually to become HQ 59th Air Depot Wing and later Northern Air Materiel Area (NAMA) finally being used by No 635 Gliding School. September 1986.

Photo: Aldon P Ferguson

277. The author standing among the rubble what was the Terminal building on Tech Site 24 August 1987. The base of the tower is to extreme right of the photograph.

Photo: Aldon P Fergu

78. A fine shot of a terrible sight! The demolition man literally knocked the terminal down with a steel ball on a crane but the reinforcement gave im more than he bargained for and it took a long time to slowly kill this once fine building which was the first and last sight of many thousands of JS servicemen and their families transiting through Burtonwood. August 1987.

Photo: Pete Boardman

279-280. On 17 April 1988 the last structure on the airfield site to the south of the main runway (and M62 motorway) was demolished. Messrs Athertons, the demolition contractors, brought in the famous chimney demolition expert Fred Dibner to undertake the final act. Fred supported one side of the tower with heavy baulks of timber and then cut away the reinforced concrete legs. After liberally covering the timber with petrol he set fire to them and as they burned they lost strength until the tower collapsed. Only a privileged few were invited to watch the last moment of this local landmark and several local people and organizations made a last minute effort to save it.

Photo: Aldon P Ferguson

281. Taken from the top of one of the floodlight towers just after demolition, this graphic photograph shows the new tower on its side with the people to the left standing on the floor of what was once hangar "J" with the base of hangar "K" behind the crane centre left. The taxiway can be seen top right pointing towards the power station and vehicles can be seen on the

BURTONWOOD 1940

Scale

1000 — 0 — 500 — 1000 — 2000 FEET

- - - - AM Boundary Shown Thus

N

To Warrington

BRD SITE

from Burtonwood

A SITE

E SITE

TECH SITE

G SITE

MARY ANN SITE

ATC

33

22

15

2

LOCATION	53 25N 02 39W	
ELEVATION	76 Ft	
RUNWAYS	04 - 22	3150 Ft
	15 - 33	3150 Ft
HANGARS	Tech Site	2 x J Type
	A Site	2 x J Type
	E Site	3 x L Type
	G Site	3 x L Type
	Mary Ann Site	3 x C Type
USERS	BRD & Mary Ann Sites	BRD Ltd
	Other Sites	No 37 MU

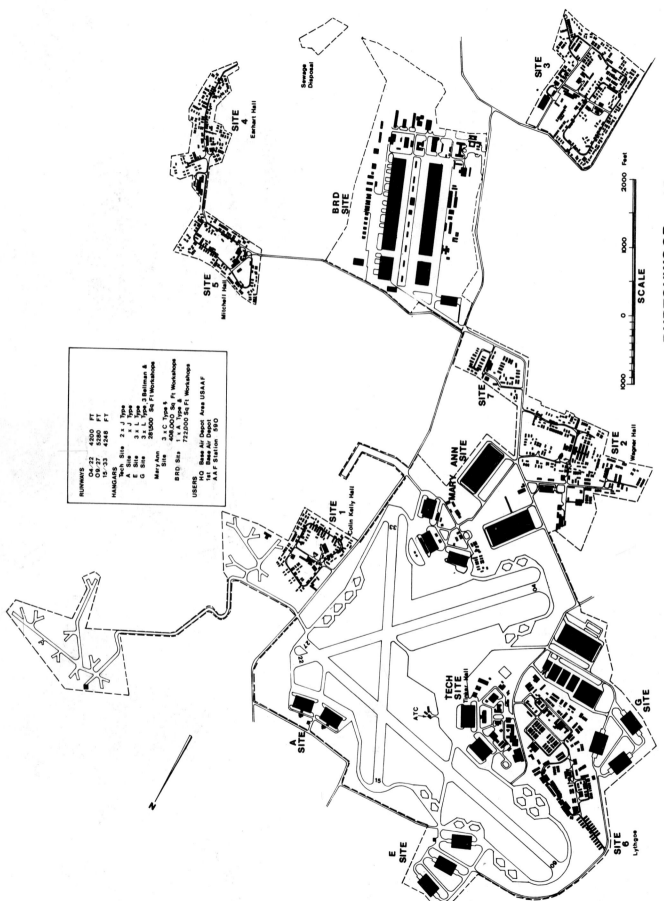

BURTONWOOD 1945

SCALE

1000   0   1000   2000   Feet

RUNWAYS
04/22   4200   FT
09/27   5280   FT
15/33   4248   FT

HANGARS
Tech. Site   2 x J Type
A Site   3 x J Type
E Site   3 x L Type
G Site   3 x L Type, 3 Bellman &
28,500 Sq Ft Workshops

Mary Ann   3 x C Type &
Site   408,000 Sq Ft Workshops

BRD Site   1 x A Type &
722,000 Sq Ft Workshops

USERS
HQ   Base Air Depot Area USAAF
1st   Base Air Depot
AAF Station 590

SITE 3

SITE 4
Earhart Hall

BRD
SITE

Sewage
Disposal

SITE
5
Mitchell Hall

SITE
7

SITE
2
Wagner Hall

SITE
1
Colin Kelly Hall

MARY ANN
SITE

TECH
SITE
Tinker Hall

ATC

A
SITE

E
SITE

G
SITE

SITE
6
Lythgoe

N

22

33

04

15

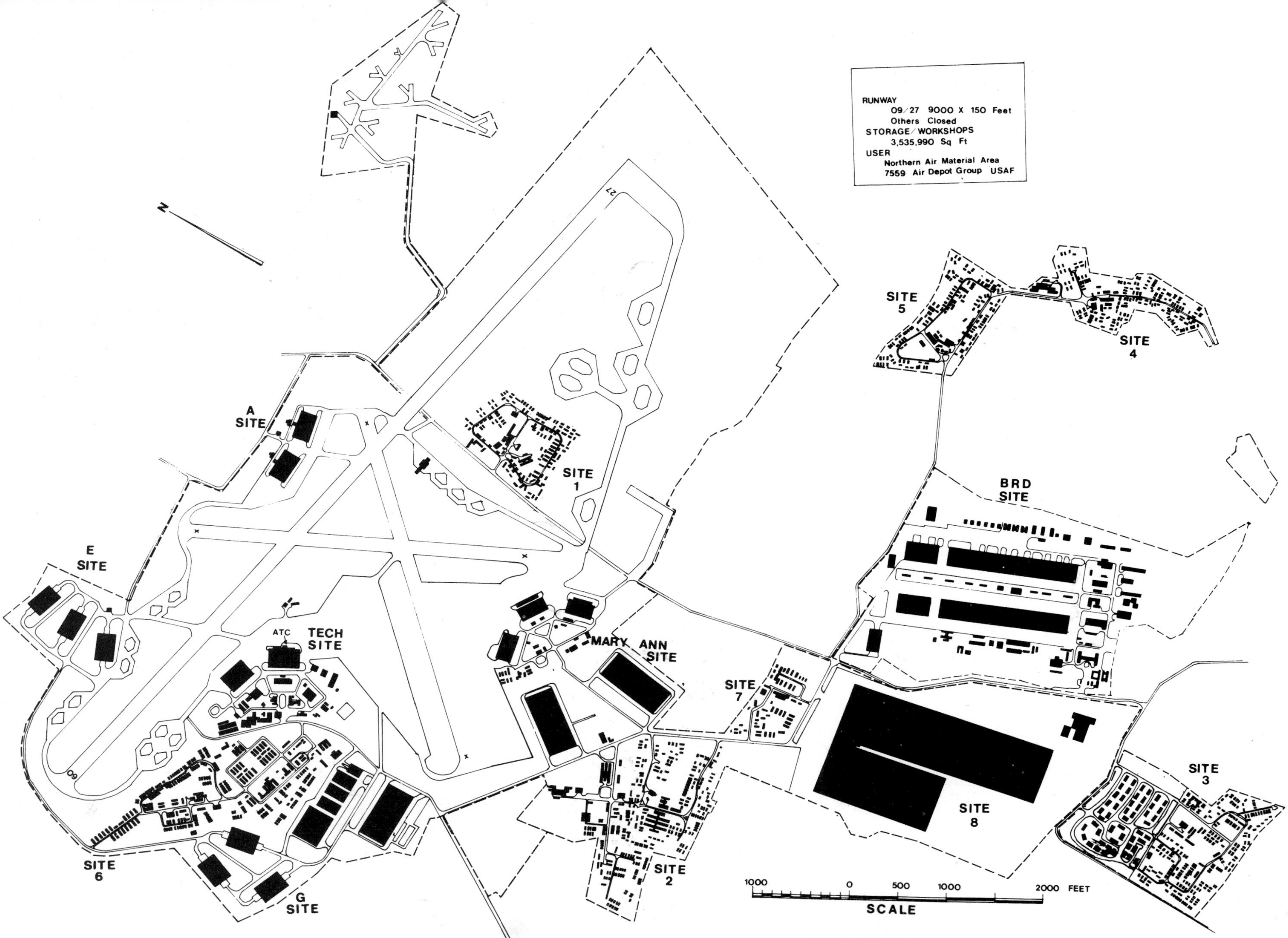

BURTONWOOD 1955

SITE 3

SITE 4

BRD SITE

SITE 5

SITE 8

SITE 7

MARY ANN SITE

SITE 2

SITE 1

SITE 6

A SITE

E SITE

TECH SITE

ATC

G SITE

RUNWAY
09.27   9000 X 150 Feet
Others   Closed
STORAGE/ WORKSHOPS
3,535,990 Sq Ft
USER
Northern Air Material Area
7559 Air Depot Group USAF

SCALE

1000   0   500   1000   2000 FEET

N

BURTONWOOD 1982

BRD SITE

SITE 3 (Living)

To Warrington

SITE 8
Header House

Helicopter Landing Area

MARY ANN SITE

TECH SITE

G SITE

M 62 MOTORWAY

From Burtonwood

MOTORWAY SERVICE AREA

M 62
From Manchester

To Liverpool

N

SCALE

1000   500   0   500   1000   1500   2000   FEET

Facts and Figures

The following schedule was prepared by Colonel William Arnold, Chief of Maitnenance Division at BAD1 and is the total production BAD1, Royal Air Force Burtonwood between 1 July 1943 and 8 May 1945.

Aircraft Assembled, Modified or Repaired

A-20	14
A-29	23
AT-6 & 16	18
B-17	4,243
B-24	694
B-25	12
B-26	444
C-45	50
C-46	6
C-47 & 53	325
C-64	16
L-1, 4 & 5	158
P-38	1,004
P-47	4,381
P-51	5
P-61	102
Mosquito	27
Other	53
Total aircraft	11,575

Aircraft Engines Overhauled

30,386

Aircraft Engine Accessories Overhauled

Sparkplugs	2,476,462
Carburettors	31,812
Magnetos	61,409
Harnesses	30,245
Cylinders	331,021

Aircraft Instruments/Accessories Overhauled/Modified

Armament

Machine guns	38,526
Solenoids	37,381
20mm cannons	836
Turrets	330
Hoist assy	984
Miscellaneous armament	261

Bombsights

Automatic pilot equipment	1,887
Stabilizers	4,521
Bombsights	2,270
Miscy bombsight equipment	5,184
K-14 gunsights & accessories	2,447

Control Surfaces

Wing & Wing tips	729
Flaps & ailerons	741
Elevators	218
Rudders	338
Horiz & vert stabilizers & fins	186
Misc wings & controls	339

Hydraulic & Tank

Wheels & brakes	4,043
Glycol heaters	7,475
Hydraulic cylinders	3,343
Hydraulic inst. & accessories	4,612
Oil temp & reg & coolers	8,462
Tanks	671
Radiator coolers	775

Paint, Dope and Fabric

Parachutes repaired & packed	71,422
Fuel cells	9,936
Life rafts	13,796
De-icers	4,586
Oxygen masks	28,394
Life vests	47,595
Control surfaces	2,194

Propeller

Propeller assemblies	11,798
Propeller blades	18,177
Propeller govenors	558
Propeller power-units	3,617

Ground & Airborne Signal Work

Radio or radar installation in a/c	13,346
Modification of existing equipment in shop	126,684
Manufacture of kits or units of equipment in shop	32,232

Modification Kits Manufactured

A-20	879
B-17	56,351
B-24	17,181
B-26	1,353
C-47	3,113
P-38	11,400
P-47	58,889
P-51	4,543
P-61	80
M-Series	355,575
Miscellaneous	458,299
L-4	471

World War II Production Figures

Date		Aircraft	Engines
Jan	1944	379	544
Feb	1944	465	724
Mar	1944	493	1,228
Apr	1944	521	1,300
May	1944	587 inc 212 B-24	1,872
June	1944	865	1,387
July	1944	914	1,534
Aug	1944	1,019	2,048
Sep	1944	782	2,207
Oct	1944	726	2,022
Nov	1944	671	1,813
Dec	1944	449	?
Jan	1945	503	2,128
Feb	1945	1,014	2,155
Mar	1945	822	?
Apr	1945	?	?
May	1945	322	?
Jun	1945	254	2,044
Jul	1945	?	Engine line closed
Aug	1945	100	
Sep	1945	100+ Scrapped 354	
Oct	onwards	Scrapping	

Base Air Depot Area (BADA)

Burtonwood (AAF 590) contained the HQ of all maintenance of aircraft and support equipment throughout the British Isles including storage and some bomb sites.

The following is a list of the bases controlled by BADA together with their compliments as at 31st March 1945.

Station	AAF No	Officers	W/O	Enl.	Total
Sudbury, Derby	158	35	4	945	984
Stansted	169	44	3	716	163
Greencastle	237	5		211	216
Constitution Hill	362	1		10	11
Bristol	473	17	1	322	340
Tostock Park	502	13	3	312	328
Liverpool	513	4		80	84
Wapley Common	515	1		10	11
St Mellons	516	1	1	40	42
Little Heathsite	517	9		180	189
Melton Mowbray	520	14		628	642
Braybrooke	521	14	2	479	495
Smethwick	522	12	5	386	403
Bures	526	4		266	270
Leicester	527			15	15
Haydock	530	5		175	180
Riseley	541	12	1	255	268
Earsham	545	14		468	482
Watford	549	20	3	150	173
Williamstrip	550	1	1	76	78
Huyton	552	22	1	571	594
Eggington, Derby	564	24	3	553	580
Poynton	571	20	1	487	508
Melchbourne	572	25	3	553	607
Wortley	581	14	1	205	220
Warton	582	256	77	8,828	9,161
Sharnbrook	583	22		457	479
Barnham	587	16	1	390	407
Burtonwood	590	495	109	15,163	15,757
Groveley Wood	592	9		268	277
Langford Lodge	597	91	15	1,121	1,227
Baverstock	802	63	4	1,687	1,754
TOTAL		1,283	229	36,033	37,545

April 1945 Facts

Value $50M, 1,823 Buildings, 2.5 miles of runway, 3.5 miles of perimeter track, 28.76 miles of road, 4.05 miles of railway track. Total Area – 1,253 acres.

4,006,852 sq ft of covered facilities comprising:
1,263,442 sq ft for Supply and Storage; 1,112,965 sq ft for Shops and Technical Operations; 1,629,445 sq ft for Administration and Housing.

7,096,181 sq ft of open facilities. Original surfaced area 781,200 sq ft. Including Canada Hall, Living Site total accommodation for 18,063 personnel.

1948 – 1958 Facts

250,000 British visitors. 800,000 cups of coffee per annum. 3,000 British cars purchased. 46,800,000 telephone calls made. 50,000 photographs taken by base photo lab. 11,000,000 miles covered by Base Motor Pool. 25,000,000 passengers carried by Base Motor Pool. 6,500 Americans married English girls. 600,000 Coca Colas served. 23,381,200 gallons of petrol consumed.

Base Contained

18 miles of surfaced roadway. 4.65 miles of railway track. 13 hangars. 1,054 nissen huts. 22 warehouses covering an area of 3,535,990 sq ft. 16.85 miles of fencing. 1,471 acres. 3,940,740 sq ft of aircraft parking apron.

The Burtonwood Association

The Burtonwood Association was formed in 1987 to maintain the records and history of the work undertaken at Burtonwood and to remember all those men and women, British and American, who have served there or have an interest in the base. Also it was established to allow ex-personnel to maintain contact with one another throughout the world and as a means of diseminating material relating to activities there throughout its history and at the present time.

Burtonwood has been an RAF base, a USAAF base, USAF base and a US Army base but has always been known as RAF Burtonwood. Today it is occupied by the 47th Area Support Group, United States Army, as a supply store for Europe.

The Association produces a quarterly twelve page newsletter entitled *Burtonwood Times* which is free to members, and annual reunions are held in the States and, so far, bi-annual ones in the UK. The first US reunion was at New Orleans in 1987, followed by Oklahoma City in 1988 and Dayton, Ohio in 1989. The first UK reunion was at Chester in June 1988 with the second in May 1990.

Anyone is welcome to join the Association; those who served there as civilians or military are entitled to full membership and interested parties may become associate members. Widows of serving personnel are also especially welcome.

For more information and an application form please write to the following:

UK	Aldon P Ferguson	USA	Thomas E Conley
	18 Ridge Way		2946 Savannah Court
	Wargrave		Waco
	Reading		TX 76710
	Berkshire RG10 8AS		USA
	England		

8th Air Force – Base Air depot – RAF Burtonwood

The definitive history of RAF Burtonwood is captured in the above book by the same author, Aldon P Ferguson. First published in 1986 this book is still available from the Publishers address at £9.25 inclusive of post and packing. The 136 pages and over 100 photographs depict the story of this famous base through World War Two, the Berlin Airlift and the support and Weather Reconnaissance operations in the 1950's, through to the current US Army occupation.